www.ingramcontent.com/pod-product-compliance
Lightning Source LLC
Chambersburg PA
CBHW080325080526
44585CB00021B/2473

37) نَجَّى – TO SAVE

COMMAND | أَنْتَ نَجِّ |

38) زَادَ – TO INCREASE

PAST

أَنْتُنَّ زِدْتُنَّ	أَنْتِ زِدْتِ	أَنْتُمْ زِدْتُمْ	أَنْتَ زِدْتَ	هُنَّ زِدْنَ
	نَحْنُ زِدْنَا	أَنَا زِدْتُ		أَنْتُمَا زِدْتُمَا

COMMAND | أَنْتَ زِدْ |

39) مَاتَ – TO DIE

PAST

أَنْتُنَّ مُتُّنَّ/ مِتُّنَّ	أَنْتِ مُتِّ/ مِتِّ	أَنْتُمْ مُتُّمْ/ مِتُّمْ	أَنْتَ مُتَّ/ مِتَّ	هُنَّ مُتْنَ/ مِتْنَ
	نَحْنُ مُتْنا/ مِتْنا	أَنَا مُتُّ/ مِتُّ		أَنْتُمَا مُتُّمَا/ مِتُّمَا

PRESENT BALD

نَحْنُ نَمُتْ	أَنَا أَمُتْ	هِيَ/أَنْتَ تَمُتْ	هُوَ يَمُتْ

40) نَسِيَ – TO FORGET

PAST | هُمْ نَسُوا |

PRESENT BALD

نَحْنُ نَنْسَ	أَنَا أَنْسَ	هِيَ/أَنْتَ تَنْسَ	هُوَ يَنْسَ

CHAPTER 1

INDEPENDENT PRONOUNS

Match each Arabic words with its definition.

ARABIC	ENGLISH
1. هُوَ	a. you all
2. أَنْتُمْ	b. both of you
3. أَنْتِ	c. you (f)
4. هُمَا	d. you all (f)
5. نَحْنُ	e. both of them
6. أَنْتُمَا	f. I
7. أَنْتَ	g. they (f)
8. هُمْ	h. you
9. هُنَّ	i. he
10. أَنَا	j. she
11. هِيَ	k. we
12. أَنْتُنَّ	l. they

Define the Arabic words without referencing anything.

1. أَنَا
2. هُمْ
3. هُمَا
4. هُوَ
5. أَنْتُمَا
6. هُنَّ

7. أَنْتُمْ
8. أَنْتُنَّ
9. أَنْتِ
10. أَنْتَ
11. نَحْنُ
12. هِيَ

[1]

ATTACHED PRONOUNS

Match each Arabic words with its definition.

ARABIC		ENGLISH	
1.	ـهُ/ـهِ	a.	you all
2.	كُمْ	b.	both of you
3.	كَ	c.	you (f)
4.	هُمَا/هِمَا	d.	you all (f)
5.	ي/نِيْ	e.	both of them
6.	كُمَا	f.	I
7.	كِ	g.	they (f)
8.	هُمْ/هِمْ	h.	you
9.	هُنَّ/هِنَّ	i.	he
10.	نَا	j.	she
11.	هَا	k.	we
12.	كُنَّ	l.	they

Define the Arabic words without referencing anything.

7. كُمْ		1. نَا	
8. كُنَّ		2. هُمْ/هِمْ	
9. كَ		3. هُمَا/هِمَا	
10. كِ		4. ـهُ/ـهِ	
11. ي/نِيْ		5. كُمَا	
12. هَا		6. هُنَّ/هِنَّ	

[2]

Highlight all pronouns in the following passage, then write the translation underneath.

عَبَسَ وَتَوَلَّىٰ ﴿١﴾ أَن جَاءَهُ الْأَعْمَىٰ ﴿٢﴾ وَمَا يُدْرِيكَ لَعَلَّهُ يَزَّكَّىٰ ﴿٣﴾ أَوْ يَذَّكَّرُ فَتَنفَعَهُ الذِّكْرَىٰ ﴿٤﴾ أَمَّا مَنِ اسْتَغْنَىٰ ﴿٥﴾ فَأَنتَ لَهُ تَصَدَّىٰ ﴿٦﴾ وَمَا عَلَيْكَ أَلَّا يَزَّكَّىٰ ﴿٧﴾ وَأَمَّا مَن جَاءَكَ يَسْعَىٰ ﴿٨﴾ وَهُوَ يَخْشَىٰ ﴿٩﴾ فَأَنتَ عَنْهُ تَلَهَّىٰ ﴿١٠﴾ كَلَّا إِنَّهَا تَذْكِرَةٌ ﴿١١﴾ فَمَن شَاءَ ذَكَرَهُ ﴿١٢﴾

CHAPTER 2
ROWS 1-2

Match each Arabic words with its definition.

ARABIC	ENGLISH
1. ءَايَة – ءَايَات	a. people
2. أَهْل/ءَال	b. book
3. عَمَل – أَعْمَال	c. deeds/work
4. نَاس	d. nation
5. قَوْم	e. messenger
6. بَيْت – بُيُوْت	f. family
7. رَسُوْل – رُسُل	g. sign
8. كِتَاب	h. house

Define the Arabic words without referencing anything.

5. عَمَل – أَعْمَال _____
6. قَوْم _____
7. رَسُوْل – رُسُل _____
8. كِتَاب _____

1. بَيْت – بُيُوْت _____
2. نَاس _____
3. أَهْل/ءَال _____
4. ءَايَة – ءَايَات _____

*Fill in the blanks, either by writing the word in **Arabic** or by using the **number** corresponding to the correct word.*

1 قَوْم	2 رَسُوْل	3 كِتَاب	4 ءَايَات	5 أَهْل	6 بُيُوْت
7 أَعْمَال	8 نَاس				

1. The _____ in this neighborhood are very expensive.

2. If I do enough good _____ I will get to heaven, God willing.

3. This _____ has so many pages.

[4]

4. There are so many _____ on this crowded street.

5. That _____ not is part of the United Nations.

6. My _____ has a big reunion every year.

7. Mother nature holds many _____ .

8. He is a _____ to all of mankind.

ROWS 3-5

Match each Arabic words with its definition.

ARABIC		ENGLISH
1. مُؤْمِن		a. liar
2. مُجْرِم		b. and
3. ال		c. criminal
4. كَافِر		d. patient one
5. صَادِق		e. oppressor
6. مُحْسِن		f. honest one
7. وَ		g. day
8. صَابِر		h. one who does good
9. يَوْم – أَيَّام		i. punishment
10. ظَالِم		j. the
11. كَاذِب		k. believer

Define the Arabic words without referencing anything.

7. صَابِر _____

8. صَادِق _____

9. عَذَاب/عِقَاب _____

10. ال _____

1. كَاذِب _____

2. وَ _____

3. يَوْم – أَيَّام _____

4. مُحْسِن _____

[5]

5. كَافِر _____   11. ظَالِم _____

6. مُؤْمِن _____   12. مُجْرِم _____

Fill in the blanks, either by writing the word in **Arabic** or by using the **number** corresponding to the correct word.

1 صَادِق	2 مُؤْمِن	3 ظَالِم	4 كَافِر	5 أَيَّام	6 عَذَاب
7 صَابِر	8 كَاذِب				

1. The nation celebrated the downfall of the _____ king.

2. This king used to issue terrible _____ for very small crimes.

3. The people who lost family under his rule were very _____ despite their grief.

4. There was a coup that lasted many _____.

5. The former king called himself a _____, but did not behave like one.

6. He made a lot of promises, but turned out to be a _____.

7. The new king is a _____, but is still more just than the old one.

8. He fulfills his promises because he is _____.

CHAPTER 3
ADJECTIVES

Match each Arabic words with its definition.

ARABIC		ENGLISH
1. كَثِيْر		a. better
2. عَلِيْم		b. near
3. شَدِيْد		c. few
4. قَرِيْب		d. far
5. كَبِيْر		e. many
6. قَلِيْل		f. knowledgeable
7. بَعِيْد		g. noble
8. عَظِيْم		h. painful
9. أَحْسَن		i. great
10. أَلِيْم		j. big
11. كَرِيْم		k. intense

Define the Arabic words without referencing anything.

7. قَلِيْل

8. شَدِيْد

9. قَرِيْب

10. كَرِيْم

11. بَعِيْد

1. أَلِيْم

2. عَظِيْم

3. كَبِيْر

4. عَلِيْم

5. كَثِيْر

6. أَحْسَن

[7]

Fill in the blanks, either by writing the word in **Arabic** or by using the **number** corresponding to the correct word.

1 قَرِيْب	2 بَعِيْد	3 كَرِيْم	4 أَحْسَن	5 كَثِيْر	6 عَلِيْم
7 كَبِيْر	8 عَظِيْم	9 أَلِيْم	10 قَلِيْل	11 شَدِيْد	

1. I can't come because my home is too _____ . If it was a bit more _____ , maybe I could make it.

2. Food portion sizes are very _____ in the US. In other countries, which is why _____ people are obese. In other countries, they eat _____ .

3. The man who wrote that book is very _____ about the subject.

4. Her face expression is always very _____ . It's scary.

5. That surgery was so _____ .

6. Even though they consider him poor and lowly, I think he is very _____ .

7. It is _____ not to talk about his issues, even if they are not secret.

8. That is _____ news!

TIME-LOCATION-DIRECTION WORDS

Match each Arabic words with its definition.

ARABIC		ENGLISH
1. قَبْلَ	a.	in
2. مِنْ	b.	with
3. عِنْدَ	c.	about/away
4. إِلَى	d.	upon
5. لِـ	e.	before
6. بِـ	f.	because/with
7. بَيْنَ	g.	after
8. عَلَى	h.	to/toward
9. عَنْ	i.	among/between
10. فِي	j.	for
11. مَعَ	k.	from
12. بَعْدَ	l.	at/near

Define the Arabic words without referencing anything.

7. بَعْدَ

8. بَيْنَ

9. لِـ

10. مَعَ

11. مِنْ

12. عَلَى

1. فِي

2. بِـ

3. عِنْدَ

4. قَبْلَ

5. إِلَى

6. عَنْ

[9]

Fill in the blanks, either by writing the word in **Arabic** or by using the **number** corresponding to the correct word.

1 قَبْلَ	2 إِلَى	3 عَنْ	4 عِنْدَ	5 مَعَ	6 فِي
7 عَلَى	8 بَعْدَ	9 بَيْنَ	10 لِ	11 مِنْ	

1. _____ I wake up each morning, my cat starts meowing. She scratches _____ the door until I come out. _____ I come out, she runs _____ her food bowl. I put food _____ her bowl and she spills it _____ the floor before eating it.

2. My husband never asks me _____ my day.

3. As a kid, he used to sleep in his parents' bed wedged _____ his mom and dad.

4. This chocolate comes _____ Belgium.

5. She eats her rice _____ ketchup.

6. These are not _____ you. Go get your own.

7. My husband never asks me _____ my day.

8. As a kid, he used to sleep in his parents' bed wedged _____ his mom and dad.

POINTERS AND SENTENCE STARTERS

Match each Arabic words with its definition.

ARABIC	ENGLISH
1. إِنَّ	a. if only
2. لَيْتَ	b. that
3. أَنَّ	c. certainly
4. لَعَلَّ	d. so that/perhaps
5. كَأَنَّ	e. however
6. لَكِنَّ	f. as though

[10]

Define the Arabic words without referencing anything.

1. إِنَّ _____   4. لَيْتَ _____

2. لَعَلَّ _____   5. كَأَنَّ _____

3. أَنَّ _____   6. لَكِنَّ _____

Point at the given words using the appropriate pointer.

| 1 هَذَا | 2 هَذِهِ | 3 هَؤُلَاءِ | 4 أُولَاءك | 5 تِلْكَ | 6 ذَلِكَ |

1. _____ lady over here.

2. _____ lady over there.

3. _____ man over here.

4. _____ man over there.

5. _____ people over there.

6. _____ people over here.

7. _____ book over there.

8. _____ man over here.

*Fill in the blanks, either by writing the word in **Arabic** or by using the **number** corresponding to the correct word.*

| 1 إِنَّ | 2 أَنَّ | 3 كَأَنَّ | 4 لَيْتَ | 5 لَكِنَّ | 6 لَعَلَّ |

1. I heard _____ you are traveling to the Maldives.

2. It is _____ she does not want to be here.

3. We missed our flight. _____ we had left a bit earlier!

4. _____, you do not actually believe that.

5. I trusted him, _____ he betrayed me.

6. If you speak more gently, _____ he may listen.

[11]

CHAPTER 4
ROWS 1-2

Match each Arabic words with its definition.

ARABIC		ENGLISH	
1.	نَفْس – أَنْفُس	a.	sky
2.	أَمْر – أُمُوْر	b.	earth
3.	حَقّ	c.	truth
4.	رَبّ	d.	path
5.	أَرْض	e.	command/matter
6.	سَبِيْل	f.	self/soul
7.	سَمَاء – سَمَوات	g.	thing
8.	شَيْء/شَيْئًا	h.	lord

Define the Arabic words without referencing anything.

5. حَقّ	_____	1. أَمْر – أُمُوْر	_____
6. رَبّ	_____	2. سَبِيْل	_____
7. نَفْس – أَنْفُس	_____	3. سَمَاء – سَمَوات	_____
8. أَرْض	_____	4. شَيْء/شَيْئًا	_____

*Fill in the blanks, either by writing the word in **Arabic** or by using the **number** corresponding to the correct word.*

1	حَقّ	2	رَبّ	3	نَفْس	4	أَرْض	5	أَمْر	6	سَبِيْل
7	سَمَاء	8	شَيْء								

1. I like to lay down on the _____ and look up at the _____.

2. Every _____ will die eventually.

3. The _____ to success is long and hard.

4. I'm telling the _____, I promise.

5. Our _____ created every _____.

6. That we pray five times a day is a _____ from our Lord.

ROWS 3-4

Match each Arabic words with its definition.

ARABIC		ENGLISH
1. جَنَّة – جَنَّات		a. heart
2. قَلْب – قُلُوْب		b. knowledge
3. يَدْ – أَيْدِي		c. fire
4. نَار		d. the last day
5. عِلْم		e. servant
6. اليَوْم الآخِر		f. reward
7. عَبْد – عِبَاد		g. hand
8. أَجْر		h. heaven/garden

Define the Arabic words without referencing anything.

5. عِلْم _____   1. أَجْر _____

6. قَلْب – قُلُوْب _____   2. نَار _____

7. جَنَّة – جَنَّات _____   3. يَدْ – أَيْدِي _____

8. اليَوْم الآخِر _____   4. عَبْد – عِبَاد _____

Fill in the blanks, either by writing the word in **Arabic** or by using the **number** corresponding to the correct word.

| 1 | أَجْر | 2 | قَلْب | 3 | يَدْ | 4 | عِلْم | 5 | عَبْد | 6 | اليَوْم الآخِر |
| 7 | نَار | 8 | جَنَّة |

1. He didn't care when she passed away. His _____ is so hard.

2. We have five fingers on each _____ .

3. There is a $5,000 _____ for whoever catches her.

4. Each person's deeds will be accounted for on _____ .

5. Atheists don't believe in _____ or _____ .

6. The name Abdullah means _____ of God.

7. Everyone loves giving their opinion, even when they have no _____ of the matter.

[14]

CHAPTER 5

ROWS 1-4

Match each Arabic words with its definition.

ARABIC		ENGLISH	
1.	قَالَ	a.	came
2.	عَلِمَ	b.	disbelieved
3.	هَدَى	c.	guided
4.	جَعَلَ	d.	sent down
5.	كَفَرَ	e.	made
6.	خَلَقَ	f.	created
7.	جَاءَ	g.	said
8.	عَمِلَ	h.	denied
9.	سَأَلَ	i.	knew
10.	كَذَّبَ	j.	did
11.	أَنْزَلَ/ نَزَّلَ	k.	asked
12.	ءامَنَ	l.	believed

Define the Arabic words without referencing anything.

1. أَنْزَلَ/ نَزَّلَ
2. جَاءَ
3. جَعَلَ
4. عَلِمَ
5. كَفَرَ
6. ءامَنَ

7. عَمِلَ
8. كَذَّبَ
9. خَلَقَ
10. هَدَى
11. قَالَ
12. سَأَلَ

Fill in the blanks, either by writing the word in **Arabic** or by using the **number** corresponding to the correct word.

| 1 قَالَ | 2 سَأَلَ | 3 ءامَنَ | 4 كَفَرَ | 5 هَدَى | 6 جَعَلَ |
| 7 جَاءَ | 8 أَنْزَلَ | 9 عَمِلَ | 10 كَذَّبَ | 11 خَلَقَ | 12 عَلِمَ |

1. He _____ so many questions. I _____ him to be quiet.

2. Allah _____ the skies and earth and _____ the Quran.

3. She used to _____ to my house every day after school.

4. Jews and Christians also _____ in God, but atheists _____.

5. My GPS _____ me when I got lost yesterday.

6. We _____ very hard for a year to open a bakery, even though we did not _____ anything about opening a business.

7. Do you _____ the fact that your factory is polluting the local river?

8. I'll _____ you the best basketball player in town.

[16]

CHAPTER 6
ACTIONS

Match each Arabic words with its definition.

ARABIC	ENGLISH
1. أَرْسَلَ	a. took
2. اتَّخَذَ	b. sent
3. عَبَدَ	c. bowed
4. سَجَدَ	d. considered
5. اتَّبَعَ	e. wronged
6. ظَلَمَ	f. worshipped
7. وَجَدَ	g. gave
8. أَخَذَ	h. found
9. ءَاتَى	i. followed

Define the Arabic words without referencing anything.

6. اتَّبَعَ   1. أَخَذَ

7. اتَّخَذَ   2. عَبَدَ

8. سَجَدَ   3. ظَلَمَ

9. وَجَدَ   4. أَرْسَلَ

                  5. ءَاتَى

*Fill in the blanks, either by writing the word in **Arabic** or by using the **number** corresponding to the correct word.*

1 أَرْسَلَ	2 أَخَذَ	3 ءَاتَى	4 عَبَدَ	5 ظَلَمَ	6 سَجَدَ
7 وَجَدَ	8 اتَّخَذَ	9 اتَّبَعَ			

1. He 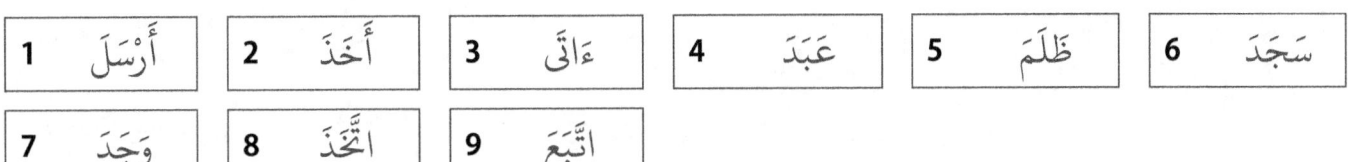 his son with freshly baked cookies to greet the new neighbors.

[17]

2. Our mom used to _____ us out to eat when she was too tired to cook.

3. They thought she had run away from home, but they _____ her under the bed.

4. Do you _____ him a friend?

5. Who do you _____ on social media?

6. In India, they still _____ idols and _____ to them.

7. I don't plan to _____ my kids an allowance.

8. Many use their power to _____ others instead of helping them.

NOUNS

Match each Arabic words with its definition.

ARABIC		ENGLISH
1. خَيْر		a. religion/judgement
2. دِيْن		b. wealth
3. مَثَل – أَمْثَال		c. bad/worse
4. قَوْل		d. deity
5. إِلَه – ءَالِهَة		e. example
6. مَال – أَمْوَال		f. angel
7. مَلَك – مَلائِكَة		g. good/better
8. شَرّ		h. speech/words

Define the Arabic words without referencing anything.

5. مَال – أَمْوَال _____

6. قَوْل _____

7. شَرّ _____

8. دِيْن _____

1. مَلَك – مَلائِكَة _____

2. خَيْر _____

3. مَثَل – أَمْثَال _____

4. إِلَه – ءَالِهَة _____

Fill in the blanks, either by writing the word in **Arabic** or by using the **number** corresponding to the correct word.

| 1 خَيْر | 2 شَرّ | 3 دِيْن | 4 قَوْل | 5 ءَالِهَة | 6 مَثَل |
| 7 مَلَائِكَة | 8 مَال |

1. I don't understand your _____. Can you give me an _____?

2. Let's stick together, for _____ or for _____.

3. Don't spend so much _____ on such useless things.

4. In their _____, they believe in multiple _____.

5. They are _____ writing down everything we do.

[19]

CHAPTER 7

NEGATION AND AFFIRMATION WORDS

Match each Arabic words with its definition.

ARABIC	ENGLISH
1. كُلّ	a. besides
2. كَلَّا	b. except
3. لَيْسَ/لا/ما	c. not...
4. إِلَّا	d. rather
5. غَيْر	e. Yes, indeed!
6. بَلْ	f. all
7. بَلَا	g. Certainly not!
8. مِنْ دُوْنِ	h. without/other than

Define the Arabic words without referencing anything.

5. إِلَّا _____   1. بَلَا _____

6. مِنْ دُوْنِ _____   2. بَلْ _____

7. لَيْسَ/لا/ما _____   3. كُلّ _____

8. غَيْر _____   4. كَلَّا _____

MORE TLDR WORDS

*Fill in the blanks, either by writing the word in **Arabic** or by using the **number** corresponding to the correct word.*

| 1 حِيْنَ/إِذْ | 2 حَتَّى | 3 تَحْتَ | 4 فَوْقَ | 5 بَعْض | 6 كَ |
| 7 مِنْ لَدُنْ | 8 وَرَاءَ/خَلْفَ | 9 بَيْنَ | 10 لِ | 11 مِنْ | |

1. _____ I grow up, I want to be a firefighter.

2. The cat is either _____ the bed or _____ the fridge.

[20]

3. He looks _____ a snake.

4. Stand in line _____ me. Don't cut. I was here first.

5. I'll try again _____ I succeed.

6. That's a gift _____ the school principal herself.

7. _____ of them use their phones in class, despite having payed $6,000 for the course.

Match each Arabic words with its definition.

ARABIC		ENGLISH	
1.	حَتَّى	a.	until
2.	كَ	b.	like
3.	بَعْض	c.	some
4.	فَوْقَ	d.	under
5.	مِنْ لَدُنْ	e.	above
6.	تَحْتَ	f.	especially from
7.	وَرَاءَ/خَلْفَ	g.	when
8.	حِيْنَ/إِذْ	h.	behind

Define the Arabic words without referencing anything.

1. كَ _____   5. حَتَّى _____

2. مِنْ لَدُنْ _____   6. تَحْتَ _____

3. وَرَاءَ/خَلْفَ _____   7. حِيْنَ/إِذْ _____

4. بَعْض _____   8. فَوْقَ _____

CHAPTER 8
QUESTION WORDS

Match each Arabic words with its definition.

ARABIC	ENGLISH
1. لَوْلا	a. why not...?
2. مَا/مَاذَا	b. where...?
3. مَنْ	c. how...?
4. أَنَّى	d. who...?
5. أَيْنَ	e. how many...?
6. كَمْ (مِنْ)	f. when...?
7. مَتَى	g. how...?!
8. أَ/هَلْ	h. is/does...?
9. أَمْ	i. or...?
10. كَيْفَ	j. what...?

Define the Arabic words without referencing anything.

6. أَ/هَلْ	_____	1. أَمْ	_____
7. أَنَّى	_____	2. كَمْ (مِنْ)	_____
8. مَتَى	_____	3. كَيْفَ	_____
9. مَنْ	_____	4. مَا/مَاذَا	_____
10. لَوْلا	_____	5. أَيْنَ	_____

*Fill in the blanks, either by writing the word in **Arabic** or by using the **number** corresponding to the correct word.*

| 1 مَتَى | 2 مَنْ | 3 كَمْ | 4 أَنَّى | 5 أَمْ | 6 كَيْفَ |
| 7 أَيْنَ | 8 أَ/هَلْ | 9 لَوْلا | 10 مَا/مَاذَا | | |

1. _____ are you looking at?

2. _____ is the tall boy standing next to you in that picture?

3. _____ do you want to go for lunch? And _____ in your lunch break?

4. _____ cupcakes are in each box?

5. _____ are you doing, sir?

6. _____ can you say such a thing?!

7. _____ you coming with us?

8. Do you prefer chicken _____ beef?

9. _____ you do what I told you to do?

ACTIONS

Match each Arabic words with its definition.

ARABIC	ENGLISH
1. كانَ	a. was pleased
2. قَتَلَ	b. was
3. أَصْبَحَ	c. killed
4. كادَ	d. became
5. اهْتَدَى	e. almost did
6. رَضِيَ	f. committed to guidance

Define the Arabic words without referencing anything.

1. رَضِيَ _____   4. كانَ _____

2. قَتَلَ _____   5. كادَ _____

3. أَصْبَحَ _____   6. اهْتَدَى _____

Fill in the blanks, either by writing the word in **Arabic** or by using the **number** corresponding to the correct word.

| 1 أَصْبَحَ | 2 كانَ | 3 اهْتَدَى | 4 رَضِيَ | 5 قَتَلَ | 6 كادَ |

1. Qaabil _____ regretful after he _____ his brother, Haabil.

2. He repented and _____, but his mother was still not _____ with him.

3. She _____ died of grief, but her husband _____ a big comfort to her during those difficult times.

CHAPTER 9

NOUNS

Match each Arabic words with its definition.

ARABIC		ENGLISH
1. مَوْت		a. sin
2. الدُّنْيا/الحَياة الدُّنْيا		b. death
3. نِعْمَة		c. life
4. حَيَاة		d. afterlife
5. الآخِرَة		e. worldly life
6. سَاعَة		f. blessing
7. إِيْمَان		g. hour
8. إِثْم/ذَنْب - ذُنُوْب		h. faith

Define the Arabic words without referencing anything.

5. مَوْت

6. حَيَاة

7. سَاعَة

8. الآخِرَة

1. نِعْمَة

2. إِيْمَان

3. إِثْم/ذَنْب - ذُنُوْب

4. الدُّنْيا/الحَياة الدُّنْيا

*Fill in the blanks, either by writing the word in **Arabic** or by using the **number** corresponding to the correct word.*

| 1 نِعْمَة | 2 مَوْت | 3 حَيَاة | 4 سَاعَة | 5 الآخِرَة | 6 الدُّنْيا |
| 7 إِيْمَان | 8 ذُنُوْب | | | | |

1. Eyesight is a big _____.

2. We should never prioritize _____ over _____.

3. The cycle of _____ and _____ that occurs in nature is a lesson for us.

[25]

4. I spend _____ working overtime every day.

5. Even people of _____ have _____.

ACTIONS

Match each Arabic words with its definition.

ARABIC		ENGLISH	
1.	أَكَلَ	a.	reached
2.	بَلَغَ	b.	looked
3.	نَظَرَ	c.	gathered
4.	حَشَرَ	d.	mentioned/remembered
5.	ذَكَرَ	e.	did
6.	فَعَلَ	f.	ate

Define the Arabic words without referencing anything.

4. أَكَلَ _____   1. نَظَرَ _____

5. فَعَلَ _____   2. ذَكَرَ _____

6. بَلَغَ _____   3. حَشَرَ _____

Fill in the blanks, either by writing the word in **Arabic** or by using the **number** corresponding to the correct word.

| 1 | نَظَرَ | 2 | بَلَغَ | 3 | فَعَلَ | 4 | أَكَلَ | 5 | ذَكَرَ | 6 | حَشَرَ |

1. When I _____ home, the first thing I do is _____.

2. My cat spends the morning _____ out the window.

3. Do you _____ when we _____ all of those pranks on the teacher in elementary school?

4. Let us _____ the children and take them outside to play.

CHAPTER 10

ALL WORDS

Match each Arabic words with its definition.

ARABIC	ENGLISH
1. وَلْـ	a. then should
2. لِـ	b. did not
3. ثُمَّ	c. then
4. فَـ	d. then/therefore/so
5. لَمْ	e. when
6. لَمَّا	f. or
7. فَلْـ	g. and should
8. أَوْ	h. should

Define the Arabic words without referencing anything.

5. ثُمَّ	_____	1. وَلْـ	_____
6. لَمَّا	_____	2. فَلْـ	_____
7. أَوْ	_____	3. لِـ	_____
8. فَـ	_____	4. أَوْ	_____

*Fill in the blanks, either by writing the word in **Arabic** or by using the **number** corresponding to the correct word.*

| 1 لِـ | 2 ثُمَّ | 3 فَـ | 4 أَوْ | 5 لَمَّا | 6 لَمْ |

1. I _____ eat breakfast today, _____ I am very hungry.

2. For lunch, I want to eat a burger _____ a sub sandwich, _____ I want ice cream for dessert.

3. _____ I skip breakfast, I spend the entire day thinking of food. I _____ eat breakfast tomorrow.

CHAPTER 11
ROWS 1-2

[27]

Match each Arabic words with its definition.

ARABIC		ENGLISH
1. خَافَ		a. promised
2. رَجَعَ		b. entered
3. سَمِعَ		c. returned
4. أَمَرَ		d. heard
5. دَخَلَ		e. feared
6. وَعَدَ		f. commanded

Define the Arabic words without referencing anything.

4. خَافَ _____   1. وَعَدَ _____

5. دَخَلَ _____   2. أَمَرَ _____

6. سَمِعَ _____   3. رَجَعَ _____

Fill in the blanks, either by writing the word in **Arabic** or by using the **number** corresponding to the correct word.

| 1 سَمِعَ | 2 رَجَعَ | 3 خَافَ | 4 أَمَرَ | 5 وَعَدَ | 6 دَخَلَ |

1. When we _____ home, let's _____ to a lecture.

2. Even though he _____ that his pet lion wouldn't hurt anyone, I still _____ that he would.

3. Didn't I _____ you not to _____ my room?

[28]

ROWS 3-4

Match each Arabic words with its definition.

ARABIC	ENGLISH
1. أَنْفَقَ	a. earned
2. غَفَرَ	b. spent
3. كَسَبَ	c. feared
4. شَاءَ	d. forgave
5. اِتَّقَى	e. associated partners
6. أَشْرَكَ	f. willed

Define the Arabic words without referencing anything.

4. شَاءَ   1. غَفَرَ

5. أَنْفَقَ   2. اِتَّقَى

6. كَسَبَ   3. أَشْرَكَ

*Fill in the blanks, either by writing the word in **Arabic** or by using the **number** corresponding to the correct word.*

| 1 أَنْفَقَ | 2 أَشْرَكَ | 3 غَفَرَ | 4 شَاءَ | 5 اتَّقَى | 6 كَسَبَ |

1. When you _____ in charity, Allah _____ your sins.

2. If he _____ he could have _____ much more money, but he decided to live simple.

3. _____ Allah and do not _____ with Him.

CHAPTER 12

CONDITIONAL WORDS + ROW 1 OF ACTIONS

Match each Arabic words with its definition.

ARABIC	ENGLISH
1. إنْ	a. loved
2. إذَا	b. provided
3. لَوْ	c. if
4. أَحَبَّ	d. misguided
5. أَضَلَّ	e. when
6. رَزَقَ	f. had

Define the Arabic words without referencing anything.

4. إذَا	1. رَزَقَ
5. أَضَلَّ	2. لَوْ
6. إنْ	3. أَحَبَّ

Fill in the blanks, either by writing the word in **Arabic** or by using the **number** corresponding to the correct word.

| 1 إنْ | 2 إذَا | 3 لَوْ | 4 أَحَبَّ | 5 أَضَلَّ | 6 رَزَقَ |

1. They said " _____ Allah _____ us with more money, we will definitely be charitable." But they are still stingy.

2. _____ you guided us, we would not have _____ .

3. It doesn't look appetizing, but _____ you taste it, you will _____ it.

ROW 2-3

Match each Arabic words with its definition.

ARABIC	ENGLISH
1. أَخْرَجَ	a. recited
2. تَلَا	b. left
3. صَبَرَ	c. judged/decreed
4. قَضَى	d. expelled/brought forth
5. نَصَرَ	e. was patient
6. خَرَجَ	f. helped

Define the Arabic words without referencing anything.

4. قَضَى   1. صَبَرَ

5. تَلَا   2. خَرَجَ

6. نَصَرَ   3. أَخْرَجَ

*Fill in the blanks, either by writing the word in **Arabic** or by using the **number** corresponding to the correct word.*

| 1 | تَلَا | 2 | صَبَرَ | 3 | نَصَرَ | 4 | أَخْرَجَ | 5 | خَرَجَ | 6 | قَضَى |

1. When her non-Muslim family heard her _____ Quran, they _____ from the house, but she was _____.

2. He _____ in favor of the criminal. I think he took a bribe.

3. An advocacy group is _____ the man who was wrongly convicted.

4. She _____ her country in pursuit of a better life.

[31]

CHAPTERS 13-15
ROWS 1-2

Match each Arabic words with its definition.

ARABIC		ENGLISH	
1.	مُبِيْن	a.	wise
2.	نَهَار	b.	night
3.	صَلَاة	c.	authoritative
4.	عَزِيْز	d.	clear
5.	لَيْل	e.	prayer
6.	رَحِيْم	f.	morning
7.	أَصْحَاب/ذُوْ	g.	merciful
8.	حَكِيْم	h.	people of...

Define the Arabic words without referencing anything.

5. نَهَار	_____	1. لَيْل	_____
6. مُبِيْن	_____	2. أُوْلُوْ	_____
7. رَحِيْم	_____	3. عَزِيْز	_____
8. حَكِيْم	_____	4. صَلَاة	_____

*Fill in the blanks, either by writing the word in **Arabic** or by using the **number** corresponding to the correct word.*

1 مُبِيْن	2 حَكِيْم	3 عَزِيْز	4 رَحِيْم	5 صَلَاة	6 أَصْحَاب/ذُوْ - أُوْلُوْ
7 لَيْل	8 نَهَار				

1. The _____ man gives very _____ explanations.

2. He works _____ and _____. What a workaholic.

3. The _____ of _____ will enter heaven though a special gate.

[32]

4. Those who are _____ to people in this life will be shown mercy in the next.

5. He speaks in an _____ way, but does not seem like a tyrant.

ROWS 3 + EXPRESSIONS OF CALLING

Match each Arabic words with its definition.

ARABIC	ENGLISH
1. نَبِي	a. pairs/spouses
2. أَزْوَاج	b. ally
3. يَا قَوْم	c. My people!
4. يَا/يَا أَيُّهَا	d. O...
5. يَا أَيُّهَا الَّذِينَ ءَامَنُوا	e. Oh Allah!
6. يَا أَيُّهَا النَّاس	f. Prophet
7. وَلِيّ	g. Oh people!
8. فَضْل	h. favor
9. رَبِّ/رَبَّنَا	i. Oh you who believe!

Define the Arabic words without referencing anything.

6. فَضْل _____

7. يَا/يَا أَيُّهَا _____

8. وَلِيّ _____

9. يَا أَيُّهَا الَّذِينَ ءَامَنُوا _____

1. يَا أَيُّهَا النَّاس _____

2. زَوْج _____

3. يَا قَوْم _____

4. نَبِيّ _____

5. رَبِّ/رَبَّنَا _____

*Fill in the blanks, either by writing the word in **Arabic** or by using the **number** corresponding to the correct word.*

1 نَبِيّ	2 أَوْلِيَاء	3 أَزْوَاج

1. At the beginning of Islam, the _____ had very few _____.

2. Male penguins are very loyal _____.

CHAPTER 16

ALL WORDS

Match each Arabic words with its definition.

ARABIC		ENGLISH	
1.	أَنْ	a.	until
2.	أَقَامَ	b.	in order to
3.	لَنْ	c.	will not
4.	تَابَ (عَلى)	d.	to
5.	لِـ(كَيْ)	e.	wanted
6.	تَابَ	f.	forgave
7.	حَتَّى	g.	repented
8.	بَعَثَ	h.	called
9.	أَرَادَ	i.	sent
10.	دَعَا	j.	established

Define the Arabic words without referencing anything.

1. بَعَثَ _____
2. تَابَ (عَلى) _____
3. تَابَ _____
4. لِـ(كَيْ) _____
5. أَرَادَ _____
6. أَنْ _____
7. أَقَامَ _____
8. لَنْ _____
9. دَعَا _____
10. حَتَّى _____

Fill in the blanks, either by writing the word in **Arabic** or by using the **number** corresponding to the correct word.

1	حَتَّى	2	لِكَيْ	3	أَنْ	4	لَنْ	5	تَابَ	6	أَقَامَ
7	أَرَادَ	8	بَعَثَ	9	دَعَا	10	تَابَ عَلَى				

1. _____ me a message when you get there _____ I can be sure that you arrived safely.

2. I hope that my kids keep _____ upon Allah on my behalf, even after I die.

3. She _____ stop throwing tantrums _____ you stop rewarding her bad behavior.

4. I want _____ visit Jerusalem one day.

5. I _____ to be from among those who _____ prayer regularly.

6. Allah _____ those who _____ sincerely.

[35]

CHAPTERS 17-19

ACTIONS

Match each Arabic words with its definition.

ARABIC		ENGLISH	
1.	جَزَى	a.	befell
2.	أَتَى	b.	revealed
3.	أَلْقَى	c.	saw
4.	أَطَاعَ	d.	compensated
5.	أَصَابَ	e.	came
6.	رَأَى	f.	cast
7.	تَوَلَّى	g.	obeyed
8.	نَادَى	h.	turned away
9.	أَوْحَى	i.	called

Define the Arabic words without referencing anything.

6. جَزَى   1. أَصَابَ

7. رَأَى   2. أَوْحَى

8. أَلْقَى   3. أَتَى

9. تَوَلَّى   4. نَادَى

                  5. أَطَاعَ

*Fill in the blanks, either by writing the word in **Arabic** or by using the **number** corresponding to the correct word.*

1 تَوَلَّى	2 أَتَى	3 رَأَى	4 أَلْقَى	5 أَوْحَى	6 جَزَى
7 أَصَابَ	8 أَطَاعَ	9 نَادَى			

1. Don't _____ from me when I'm talking to you!

[36]

2. Children should _____ their parents unless their parents are requesting something bad or unreasonable.

3. If you are patient when a calamity _____ you, you will be _____ well for your patience.

4. My cat never _____ when I _____ him

5. He claims that it was _____ to him that he should be using donor money to fly first class. Says he _____ it in a dream. I smell a fraud.

6. He _____ the ball so hard, he tore his rotator cuff.

NOUNS

Match each Arabic words with its definition.

ARABIC		ENGLISH	
1.	وُجُوْه	a.	fathers
2.	يَوْمَئِذٍ	b.	humans
3.	ءَابَاء	c.	on that day
4.	مَاء	d.	water
5.	عَالَمِيْنَ	e.	faces
6.	إِنْسَان	f.	the day of standing
7.	يَوْمَ القِيَامَةِ	g.	creation
8.	أَحَد/وَاحِد	h.	one

Define the Arabic words without referencing anything.

1. وَجْه _____   5. عَالَمِيْن _____

2. يَوْمَ القِيَامَة _____   6. وَاحِد/أَحَد _____

3. يَوْمَئِذٍ _____   7. إِنْسَان _____

4. ءَابَاء _____   8. مَاء _____

[37]

Fill in the blanks, either by writing the word in **Arabic** or by using the **number** corresponding to the correct word.

1 أَحَد	2 عَالَمِيْن	3 إِنْسَان	4 وَجْه	5 مَاء	6 يَوْم القِيامة
7 يَومَئِذٍ	8 ءَابَاء				

1. Wash your _____ with _____. You look sleepy.

2. Not _____ of them will question the beliefs of their _____.

3. All of _____ will be gathered on _____.

4. Every _____ has the basic right to food, shelter, clothing, and water.

5. _____ we will face our accounting.

[38]

CHAPTER 20

ROWS 1-2

Match each Arabic words with its definition.

ARABIC		ENGLISH	
1. أَنْذَرَ		a.	taught
2. عَلَّمَ		b.	forbade
3. حَرَّمَ		c.	destroyed
4. أَهْلَكَ		d.	fabricated
5. أَدْخَلَ		e.	admitted
6. اِفْتَرَى		f.	warned

Define the Arabic words without referencing anything.

4. أَهْلَكَ _____

5. أَنْذَرَ _____

6. أَدْخَلَ _____

1. اِفْتَرَى _____

2. حَرَّمَ _____

3. عَلَّمَ _____

*Fill in the blanks, either by writing the word in **Arabic** or by using the **number** corresponding to the correct word.*

| 1 أَدْخَلَ | 2 أَنْذَرَ | 3 أَهْلَكَ | 4 افْتَرَى | 5 عَلَّمَ | 6 حَرَّمَ |

1. He does not _____ a nation before He _____ them.

2. Can you _____ me Arabic, please?

3. Is it true that alcohol is _____ in your religion?

4. They _____ lies against her to get revenge

5. Don't _____ strangers into the house, genius.

[39]

ROWS 3-4

Match each Arabic words with its definition.

ARABIC		ENGLISH	
1.	أَحْيَى	a.	pondered
2.	اِسْتَطَاعَ	b.	sought forgiveness
3.	اِسْتَغْفَرَ	c.	was arrogant
4.	تَوَكَّلَ	d.	was able
5.	تَذَكَّرَ	e.	gave life
6.	اِسْتَكْبَرَ	f.	relied

Define the Arabic words without referencing anything.

4. تَوَكَّلَ _____

5. اِسْتَكْبَرَ _____

6. أَحْيَى _____

1. تَذَكَّرَ _____

2. اِسْتَطَاعَ _____

3. اِسْتَغْفَرَ _____

*Fill in the blanks, either by writing the word in **Arabic** or by using the **number** corresponding to the correct word.*

| 1 تَذَكَّرَ | 2 تَوَكَّلَ | 3 أَحْيَى | 4 اِسْتَغْفَرَ | 5 اِسْتَكْبَرَ | 6 اِسْتَطَاعَ |

1. When spring comes after a long winter, you should _____ how God _____ after death.

2. Tough situations help you learn how to _____ on Allah.

3. He was not _____ to ask questions in class because of his pride. He _____

4. It can be tough to admit that you were wrong and to _____.

[40]

CHAPTER 21
ALL WORDS

Match each Arabic words with its definition.

ARABIC		ENGLISH	
1.	بَشَر	a.	like
2.	صَالِح – صَالِحَات	b.	magic
3.	وَيْل	c.	outcome
4.	صَدْر – صُدُور	d.	first/earliest
5.	بَيِّنَة – بَيِّنَات	e.	woe
6.	عَاقِبَة	f.	chest
7.	سِحْر	g.	home
8.	جَمِيع/أَجْمَعِيْن	h.	witness
9.	دَار – دِيَار	i.	all
10.	شَهِيْد – شُهَدَاء	j.	clear proof
11.	أَوَّل	k.	good/good deeds
12.	مِثْل	l.	human

Define the Arabic words without referencing anything.

7. مِثْل

8. عَاقِبَة

9. دَار – دِيَار

10. سِحْر

11. صَالِح – صَالِحَات

12. شَهِيْد – شُهَدَاء

1. بَيِّنَة – بَيِّنَات

2. صَدْر – صُدُور

3. بَشَر

4. جَمِيع/أَجْمَعِيْن

5. أَوَّل

6. وَيْل

[41]

Fill in the blanks, either by writing the word in **Arabic** or by using the **number** corresponding to the correct word.

1 بَشَر	2 مِثْل	3 سِحْر	4 عَاقِبَة	5 وَيْل	6 أَوَّل
7 أَجْمَعِيْن	8 دَار	9 صَدْر	10 صَالِحَات	11 بَيِّنَات	12 شَهِيْد

1. He was the _____ person to do _____ tricks in front of an audience.

2. The _____ came to court with _____, but his testimony was still rejected. How unjust!

3. The disbelievers say, "He is a _____ just _____ us. He is not an angel. Why should we accept him as a prophet?"

4. We must all face the _____ of our actions.

5. Why did he invite the poor person into his _____? Maybe he's just trying to do _____?

6. During an open heart surgery, they break open your _____.

7. The entire family when for a picnic _____. No one was left behind.

8. _____ to you!

[42]

CHAPTER 22

ADJECTIVES AND NOUNS

Match each Arabic words with its definition.

ARABIC		ENGLISH	
1.	رَحْمَة	a.	forgiving
2.	سَلام	b.	capable
3.	الرَّحْمٰن	c.	seeing
4.	غَفُوْر	d.	the Most Merciful
5.	بَصِيْر	e.	mercy
6.	خَبِيْر	f.	hearing
7.	سَمِيْع	g.	informed
8.	قَدِيْر	h.	peace

Define the Arabic words without referencing anything.

5. قَدِيْر   1. رَحْمَة

6. الرَّحْمٰن   2. خَبِيْر

7. بَصِيْر   3. غَفُوْر

8. سَلام   4. سَمِيْع

*Fill in the blanks, either by writing the word in **Arabic** or by using the **number** corresponding to the correct word.*

1 قَدِيْر	2 سَمِيْع	3 خَبِيْر	4 بَصِيْر	5 غَفُوْر	6 الرَّحْمٰن
7 سَلام	8 رَحْمَة				

1. You're so cruel. Are you even _____ of showing _____ ?

2. Parents who are not well- _____ about the culture that their kids are growing up with can't connect well with them.

[43]

3. I offer you greetings of _____.

4. Don't worry about what people will say. Worry about the opinion of the one who is most _____ and _____.

5. There is a famous surah by the name of _____. Why do people love it so much?

6. Don't despair. He is very _____.

ACTIONS

Match each Arabic words with its definition.

ARABIC		ENGLISH
1. مَسَّ		a. strayed
2. صَدَّ		b. touched
3. رَدَّ		c. averted
4. ضَلَّ		d. saved
5. نَجَّى		e. thought
6. ظَنَّ		f. returned

Define the Arabic words without referencing anything.

4. ضَلَّ _____

5. مَسَّ _____

6. صَدَّ _____

1. نَجَّى _____

2. ظَنَّ _____

3. رَدَّ _____

[44]

Fill in the blanks, either by writing the word in **Arabic** or by using the **number** corresponding to the correct word.

| 1 ظَنَّ | 2 ضَلَّ | 3 مَسَّ | 4 صَدَّ | 5 رَدَّ | 6 نَجَّى |

1. Why would you _____ that it's okay to _____ me like that? Keep your hands to yourself.

2. I have _____ from the tour group and I can't find them. Please, _____ me.

3. You stole that from her. _____ it immediately.

4. They used to _____ people from Islam by telling them that the Prophet was a magician that would destroy their families if they listened to him.

CHAPTER 23

ALL WORDS

Match each Arabic words with its definition.

ARABIC		ENGLISH
1. سُلْطان	a.	God consciousness
2. حَمْد	b.	testimony
3. سُوْء	c.	Glory be to…
4. فِتْنَة	d.	authority
5. ضَلال	e.	wisdom
6. شَهادَة	f.	trial
7. مِيْثاق	g.	evil
8. مُلْك	h.	ownership
9. سُبْحان	i.	permission
10. حِكْمَة	j.	praise
11. إِذْن	k.	covenant
12. تَقْوَى	l.	misguidance

Define the Arabic words without referencing anything.

7. تَقْوَى

8. ضَلال

9. شَهادَة

10. فِتْنَة

11. حَمْد

12. سُبْحان

1. مُلْك

2. إِذْن

3. سُلْطان

4. سُوْء

5. مِيْثاق

6. حِكْمَة

Fill in the blanks, either by writing the word in **Arabic** or by using the **number** corresponding to the correct word.

1 تَقْوَى	2 سُلْطَان	3 إِذْن	4 حَمْد	5 شَهَادَة	6 حِكْمَة
7 مُلْك	8 مِيثَاق	9 سُبْحَان	10 فِتْنَة	11 سُوْء	12 ضَلَال

1. You do not have the _____ to do that. You must get _____ from the board.

2. Don't shower him with _____. He'll get a big head.

3. She has a lot of _____ considering her age. She always makes very good decisions.

4. If you break your _____, I won't hesitate to provide _____ against you in court. It's only fair.

5. Difficult _____ can help build your _____.

6. He gained _____ of those assets through very _____ means.

7. You never know when someone deep in _____ will come back.

8. _____ God!

[47]

CHAPTER 24

ALL WORDS

Match each Arabic words with its definition.

ARABIC		ENGLISH	
1.	الَّذِيْ	a.	what/whatever
2.	الَّذِيْنَ	b.	either... or
3.	الَّتِيْ	c.	only
4.	مَا	d.	from what
5.	مَنْ	e.	the one who (f)
6.	بِمَا	f.	with regards to what
7.	عَمَّا	g.	whenever
8.	فِيْمَا	h.	as for
9.	مِمَّا	i.	just as
10.	كَمَا	j.	because of
11.	كُلَّمَا	k.	the one who
12.	إِنَّمَا	l.	one who/whoever
13.	أَنَّمَا	m.	the ones who
14.	أَمَّا	n.	that
15.	إِمَّا	o.	about what

Define the Arabic words without referencing anything.

1. كَمَا _____
2. مَا _____
3. الَّذِيْنَ _____
4. مِمَّا _____
5. كُلَّمَا _____
6. فِيْمَا _____
7. بِمَا _____
8. الَّتِيْ _____

9. إِمَّا _____
10. أَنَّمَا _____
11. عَمَّا _____
12. إِنَّمَا _____
13. الَّذِيْ _____
14. أَمَّا _____
15. مَنْ _____

[49]

CHAPTER 25

NOUNS

Match each Arabic words with its definition.

ARABIC		ENGLISH	
1.	قَمَر	a.	child
2.	رِجَال	b.	woman
3.	شَمْس	c.	brothers
4.	امْرَأة	d.	moon
5.	حِسَاب	e.	sun
6.	إِخْوَان	f.	nation
7.	أُمَّة	g.	men
8.	أَبْنَاء	h.	accounting

Define the Arabic words without referencing anything.

5. إِخْوَان   1. أُمَّة

6. امْرَأة   2. أَبْنَاء

7. شَمْس   3. رِجَال

8. قَمَر   4. حِسَاب

*Fill in the blanks, either by writing the word in **Arabic** or by using the **number** corresponding to the correct word.*

| 1 | أَبْنَاء | 2 | إِخْوَان | 3 | امْرَأة | 4 | رِجَال | 5 | قَمَر | 6 | شَمْس |
| 7 | حِسَاب | 8 | أُمَّة |

1. I'm the only _____ in my house. I have four _____ and no daughters. Even growing up, I had five _____ and no sisters.

2. Which do you think is more beautiful, the _____ or the _____ ?

[50]

3. On the day of _____, each prophet will stand with his _____.

4. You see a lot of _____ with beards nowadays. It seems to be in fashion.

ACTIONS

Match each Arabic words with its definition.

ARABIC	ENGLISH
1. عَقَلَ	a. forgot
2. نَسِيَ	b. died
3. شَكَرَ	c. wrote/decreed
4. كَتَبَ	d. reasoned
5. مَاتَ	e. increased
6. زَادَ	f. was grateful

Define the Arabic words without referencing anything.

4. شَكَرَ _____   1. زَادَ _____

5. مَاتَ _____   2. كَتَبَ _____

6. نَسِيَ _____   3. عَقَلَ _____

| 1 شَكَرَ | 2 زَادَ | 3 عَقَلَ | 4 نَسِيَ | 5 مَاتَ | 6 كَتَبَ |

1. If you _____, Allah will _____ your blessings.

2. It took 6 months to _____ this book.

3. Use your brain. Why don't you _____ through the problem.

4. After he _____ and was buried, he was _____.

CHAPTER 26

NOUNS

Match each Arabic words with its definition.

ARABIC	ENGLISH
1. نُوْر	a. sea
2. ظُلُمَات	b. child
3. بَحْر	c. warner
4. غَيْب	d. light
5. جِبَال	e. darkness
6. وَلَد	f. town
7. نَذِيْر	g. unseen
8. قَرْيَة	h. mountains

Define the Arabic words without referencing anything.

5. ظُلُمَات _____

6. نُوْر _____

7. وَلَد _____

8. غَيْب _____

1. بَحْر _____

2. جِبَال _____

3. نَذِيْر _____

4. قَرْيَة _____

Fill in the blanks, either by writing the word in **Arabic** or by using the **number** corresponding to the correct word.

| 1 غَيْب | 2 وَلَد | 3 قَرْيَة | 4 نَذِيْر | 5 جِبَال | 6 بَحْر |
| 7 ظُلُمَات | 8 نُوْر | | | | |

1. In the Quran, misguidance and guidance after often compared to _____ and _____ .

2. Send a _____ with the message that the _____ is under attack!

[52]

3. Would you prefer to live high up in the _____ or right by the _____ ?

4. No human has knowledge of the _____ .

5. He has a lot of responsibilities even though he is just a _____ .

ACTIONS

Match each Arabic words with its definition.

ARABIC	ENGLISH
1. عَذَّبَ	a. informed
2. حَسِبَ	b. judged
3. شَهِدَ	c. punished
4. حَكَّمَ	d. thought
5. نَبَّأَ	e. witnessed
6. سَبَّحَ	f. declared perfect

Define the Arabic words without referencing anything.

1. نَبَّأَ _____   4. شَهِدَ _____

2. سَبَّحَ _____   5. عَذَّبَ _____

3. حَكَّمَ _____   6. حَسِبَ _____

Fill in the blanks, either by writing the word in **Arabic** or by using the **number** corresponding to the correct word.

| 1 شَهِدَ | 2 حَسِبَ | 3 حَكَّمَ | 4 سَبَّحَ | 5 عَذَّبَ | 6 نَبَّأَ |

1. Why didn't you _____ me of this important new earlier?

2. She _____ the death of her own grandmother when they were living in a war zone. She was so traumatized, I _____ she would never speak again.

3. He always _____ very fairly. He does not accept bribes and he is thorough in his research.

4. So many people are _____ unjustly in this legal system.

5. We _____ God during each prayer.

IRREGULAR ACTION INDEX

© Nusayba and Sumaya Al-Saadoon, 2018

No-Nonsense Arabic: A Practical, To-The-Point Program for Understanding the Arabic of the Quran - Vocabulary

All rights reserved. This book or any portion thereof may not be reproduced, stored in a retrieval system, or transmitted in any form by any means without the express written permission of Nusayba and Sumaya Al-Saadoon.

For comments/questions contact us at no.nonsense.arabic@gmail.com

For more information visit www.qurancoach.org

ISBN: 978-1-7324585-2-9

A GUIDE TO THE VOCABULARY

METHODOLOGY

- All words contained within this packet **appear frequently** in the Quran

- The words contained within this packet make up **85% of the Quran**

- Included with each set of words is:

    - **A FREQUENCY COUNT** – the number of times a set of words appears in the Quran

    - **A PERCENTAGE TRACKER** – the percentage of the Quran that these words make up

- Chapters 9 -23 include a **set phrase** or an expression. These set phrases are not included in the percentage count.

- The words are **sorted based on frequency and relevance** to the concepts covered in a given chapter.

- This packet includes **exercises for each chapter** that will help you memorize the vocabulary. The exercises begin **after** the Ch.26 vocabulary.

SYMBOLS AND ANNOTATIONS

- A **dash (-)** between words means that the first is **singular** and the second is **plural**. Remember that Arabic is read from right to left.

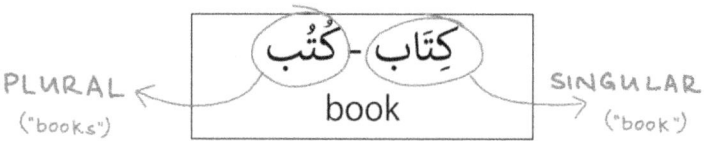

✧ If there is only one word in the box it either means that there is no plural or that the plural is not commonly used in the Quran.

- A **slash (/)** between words indicates that the two words are **synonyms**.

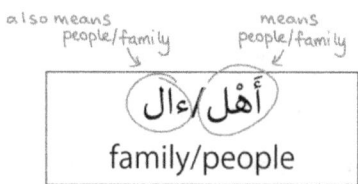

- A **numeral superscript (¹, ², ³, etc.)** is used to mark **irregular actions**. Refer to the appendix for relevant charts for all irregular actions.

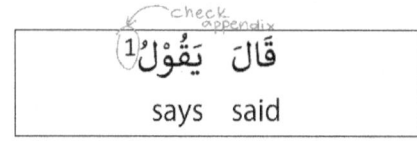

CHAPTER 01
VOCABULARY

INDEPENDENT PRONOUNS

Pronouns are the most important commonly used words you'll learn. They are EVERYWHERE. That is why they are our first set of vocabulary words. Memorizing your pronouns is vital!

أَنْتُنَّ	أَنْتِ		هُنَّ	هِيَ		أَنْتُمْ	أَنْتَ		هُمْ	هُوَ
you all (f)	you (f)		they (f)	she/it/they		you all	you		they	he/it

		أَنْتُما		هُما		نَحْنُ	أَنا
		both of you		both of them		we	I

ATTACHED PRONOUNS

The pronouns below attach to the ends of words, unlike their independent counterparts listed above. We will come to understand the usage of the two types of pronouns more clearly in the chapters to come.

كُنَّ	كِ		هُنَّ/هِنَّ	هَا		كُمْ	كَ		هُمْ/هِمْ	هُ/هِ
you all (f)	you (f)		they (f)	she/it/they		you all	you		they	he/it

		كُما		هُما/هِما		نا	يَ/نِي
		both of you		both of them		we	I

WHERE ARE WE AT?	
# OF OCCURRENCES:	~12,070
% COVERED:	15%

CHAPTER 02
VOCABULARY

COMMON NOUNS

Here are ten common nouns that will allow us to dive into some basic translation!

عَمَل - أَعْمَال deed/work	رَسُوْل - رُسُل messenger	كِتَاب - كُتُب book/record	ءَايَة - ءَايَات sign
نَاس people	بَيْت - بُيُوْت house	أَهْل/ءَال family/people	قَوْم nation
وَ and	الْـ the	يَوْم - أَيَّام day	عَذَاب/عِقَاب punishment

WHERE ARE WE AT?
OF OCCURRENCES: ~3,015*
% COVERED: 19%

*excluding وَ and الْـ

HYBRID WORDS

These words can be used both as nouns or description.
Note that all nouns that refer to humans can be made feminine by adding a ة. A female believer, for example, is a مُؤْمِنَة.

كَاذِب - كَاذِبُوْنَ lying/liar	صَادِق - صَادِقُوْنَ honest/honest one	كَافِر - كَافِرُوْنَ/كُفَّار disbelieving/disbeliever	مُؤْمِن - مُؤْمِنُوْنَ believing/believer
مُجْرِم – مُجْرِمُوْنَ criminal	مُحْسِن - مُحْسِنُوْنَ one who does good	ظَالِم - ظَالِمُوْنَ oppressive/oppressor	صَابِر - صَابِرُوْنَ patient/patient one

WHERE ARE WE AT?
OF OCCURRENCES: ~730
% COVERED: 20%

CHAPTER 03
VOCABULARY

COMMON ADJECTIVES

An adjective, also known as a descriptor, is a word used to describe a noun.

أَلِيْم	شَدِيْد	قَرِيْب	بَعِيْد
painful	intense	near	far

عَظِيْم	كَبِيْر	قَلِيْل	كَثِيْر
great	big	few	many

	أَحْسَن	عَلِيْم	كَرِيْم
	better	knowledgeable	noble

WHERE ARE WE AT?
OF OCCURRENCES: ~695
% COVERED: 21%

COMMON TIME-LOCATION-DIRECTION WORDS

Here are the most common TLD words in the Quran. More to come later!

فِيْ	عَلَى	إِلَى	مِنْ
in	upon	to/towards	from

مَعَ	عَنْ	بِـ	لِـ
with	about/away	with/because	for (possessive)

عِنْدَ	بَيْنَ	بَعْدَ	قَبْلَ
at/near	among/between	after	before

WHERE ARE WE AT?
OF OCCURRENCES: ~9,780
% COVERED: 34%

POINTERS

Pointers can appear as part of a pointer fragment (this book), but also outside of one (This is a book).

تِلْكَ	ذَلِكَ	هَذِهِ	هَذا
that (f)/those	that	this (f)/these	this

		أُوْلَاءِكَ	هَؤُلَاءِ
		those (people)	these (people)

WHERE ARE WE AT?
OF OCCURRENCES: ~1,050
% COVERED: 35%

SENTENCE STARTERS

Remember that a sentence starter acts an auxiliary feature – if you remove it, you will still have a full sentence.

لَكِنَّ	كَأَنَّ	أَنَّ	إِنَّ
however	as though	that	certainly/no doubt

		لَعَلَّ	لَيْتَ
		so that/perhaps	if only

WHERE ARE WE AT?
OF OCCURRENCES: ~2,300
% COVERED: 38%

CHAPTER 04
VOCABULARY

NOUNS

نَفْس - أَنْفُس self/soul	أَرْض earth	سَمَاء - سَمَوات sky	رَبّ lord
أَمْر - أُمُوْر matter/command	سَبِيْل path	حَقّ truth	شَيْء/شَيْئًا* thing/at all
اليَوْم الآخِر the last day	عَبْد - عِباد servant	جَنَّة - جَنَّات garden/heaven	نَار fire
قَلْب - قُلُوْب heart	عِلْم knowledge	أَجْر reward	يَد - أَيْدِيْ hand

*when شيء/من شيء/شيئا appears in a negated sentence, it will usually have the meaning of "at all".
We will learn more about negation in Chapter 7.

WHERE ARE WE AT?	
# OF OCCURRENCES:	~3,505
% COVERED:	43%

CHAPTER 05
VOCABULARY

ACTIONS

These 12 actions are most common in the Quran, each averaging at 335 occurrences!

يَجْعَلُ	جَعَلَ		يَعْمَلُ	عَمِلَ		يَعْلَمُ	عَلِمَ
makes	made		does	did		knows	knew

يَكْفُرُ	كَفَرَ		يَخْلُقُ	خَلَقَ		يَسْأَلُ	سَأَلَ
disbelieves	disbelieved		creates	created		asks	asked

يُنْزِلُ/يُنَزِّلُ	أَنْزَلَ/نَزَّلَ		يَجِيْءُ[2]	جَاءَ		يَقُوْلُ[1]	قَالَ
sends down	sent down		comes	came		says	said

يُكَذِّبُ	كَذَّبَ		يَهْدِي[3]	هَدَى		يُؤْمِنُ	ءَامَنَ
denies	denied		guides	guided		believes	believed

WHERE ARE WE AT?	
# OF OCCURRENCES:	~4,010
% COVERED:	48%

CHAPTER 06
VOCABULARY

ACTIONS

يُرْسِلُ	أَرْسَلَ
sends	sent

يَتَّبِعُ	اتَّبَعَ
follows	followed

يُؤْتِي	ءَاتَى [4]
gives	gave

يَعْبُدُ	عَبَدَ
worships	worshipped

يَتَّخِذُ	اتَّخَذَ
considers	considered

يَأْخُذُ [5]	أَخَذَ
takes	took

يَسْجُدُ	سَجَدَ
bows	bowed

يَجِدُ	وَجَدَ
finds	found

يَظْلِمُ	ظَلَمَ
wrongs	wronged

WHERE ARE WE AT?
OF OCCURRENCES: ~1,135
% COVERED: 49.5%

NOUNS

Once you memorize these 8 words, you'll have reached the half way point!

دِيْن
religion/judgement

إِلَه - ءَالِهَة
deity

شَرّ
bad/worse

خَيْر
good/better

قَوْل
speech/words

مَال - أَمْوَال
wealth

مَثَل - أَمْثَال
example

مَلَك - مَلَائِكَة
angel

WHERE ARE WE AT?
OF OCCURRENCES: ~800
% COVERED: 50.5%

CHAPTER 07
VOCABULARY

NEGATION AND AFFIRMATION WORDS

غَيْر	مِنْ دُوْنِ	كَلَّا	لَا/مَا/لَيْسَ
other than/without	besides/other than	Certainly not!	not...

بَلَى	بَلْ	إِلَّا	كُلّ*
Yes, indeed!	rather	except	all

*كُلّ often appears as the first word in a possessive fragment (all **of**...). Unlike like what we have seen before, the second word will often be general as opposed to specific (i.e., كُلُّ شَيْءٍ = all things/every thing).

WHERE ARE WE AT?	
# OF OCCURRENCES:	~4,500
% COVERED:	56%

MORE TIME-LOCATION-DIRECTION

Though the TLD words you were introduced to it Ch. 3 are the most common, there are more.

فَوْقَ	تَحْتَ	بَعْض*	وَرَاءَ/خَلْفَ
above	under	some/each other	behind

حَتَّى	كَ**	حِيْنَ/إِذْ	مِنْ لَدُنْ
until	like	when	(especially) from

*note that بعض is the only word in this table that is not a TLD word (it does not denote time, place, or direction). It usually appears as the first word in a possessive fragment (some **of**...)

**كَ always attaches directly to the beginning of a word (كَالْأَرْضِ = like the earth)

WHERE ARE WE AT?	
# OF OCCURRENCES:	~740
% COVERED:	57%

CHAPTER 08
VOCABULARY

QUESTION WORDS

These question words appear at the beginning of both is sentences and action sentences. They do not disrupt the sentence structure in Arabic. In English, you may need to do some shifting of the order of the words.

أَهَلْ	مَا/مَاذَا	مَتَى	كَيْفَ
is/does···?	what···?	when···?	how···?

كَمْ (مِنْ)	مَنْ	أَيْنَ	أَنَّى
how many···?	who···?	where···?	how···?!?

أَمْ	لَوْلَا
or···?	why not···?

WHERE ARE WE AT?	
# OF OCCURRENCES:	~550
% COVERED:	58%

ACTIONS

كان is the most common of these four words, and accounts for a very large percent of this number.

گَادَ	يَكَادُ[7]	أَصْبَحَ	يُصْبِحُ	كَانَ	يَكُوْنُ[6]
almost did	almost does	became	becomes	was	is/be

رَضِيَ	يَرْضَى[9]	اِهْتَدَى	يَهْتَدِيْ[8]	قَتَلَ	يَقْتُلُ
was pleased	is pleased	committed to guidance	commits to guidance	killed	kills

WHERE ARE WE AT?	
# OF OCCURRENCES:	~1,480
% COVERED:	60%

CHAPTER 09
VOCABULARY

NOUNS

حَيَاة	life
مَوْت	death
الآخِرَة	the afterlife
الدُّنْيَا/الحَيَاة الدُّنْيَا	the worldly life
إِثْم/ذَنْب - ذُنُوْب	sin
نِعْمَة	blessing
إِيْمَان	faith
سَاعَة	hour

WHERE ARE WE AT?	
# OF OCCURRENCES:	~605
% COVERED:	61.5%

ACTIONS

Past	Present	Meaning
نَظَرَ	يَنْظُرُ	looked / looks
فَعَلَ	يَفْعَلُ	did / does
أَكَلَ	يَأْكُلُ [10]	ate / eats
حَشَرَ	يَحْشُرُ	gathered / gathers
بَلَغَ	يَبْلُغُ	reached / reaches
ذَكَرَ	يَذْكُرُ	remembered / remembers; mentioned / mentions

WHERE ARE WE AT?	
# OF OCCURRENCES:	~430
% COVERED:	62%

SET PHRASES

جَنَّات تَجْرِي مِنْ تَحْتِها الأَنْهَارُ	gardens under which rivers flow

CHAPTER 10
VOCABULARY

SHAVING WORDS

These words only ever appear before present tense actions. They cause the ـَ at the end to be replaced with a ـْ or causing the ن to drop.

فَلْ	وَلْ	لِ	لَمْ
then should	and should	should	did not

WHERE ARE WE AT?
OF OCCURRENCES: ~1,080
% COVERED: 63%

COMMON WORDS

لَمَّا	أَوْ	ثُمَّ	فَ
when	or	then	then/therefore/so

WHERE ARE WE AT?
OF OCCURRENCES: ~3,775
% COVERED: 68%

SET PHRASES

خَالِدِينَ فِيْها (أَبَدًا)
remaining therein (forever)

CHAPTER 11

VOCABULARY

ACTIONS

يَسْمَعُ	سَمِعَ
hears	heard

يَرْجِعُ	رَجَعَ
returns	returned

يَخَافُ[11]	خَافَ
fears	feared

يَعِدُ	وَعَدَ
promises	promised

يَدْخُلُ	دَخَلَ
enters	entered

يَأْمُرُ	أَمَرَ
commands	commanded

يَكْسِبُ	كَسَبَ
earns	earned

يَغْفِرُ	غَفَرَ
forgives	forgave

يُنْفِقُ	أَنْفَقَ
spends	spent

يُشْرِكُ	أَشْرَكَ
associates partners	associated partners

يَتَّقِي[13]	اتَّقَى
is conscious of God	was conscious of God

يَشَاءُ[12]	شَاءَ
wills	willed

WHERE ARE WE AT?
OF OCCURRENCES: ~1,110
% COVERED: 70%

SET PHRASES

بَنِي إِسْرَائِيل
the children of Israel
(the descendants of the 12 sons of Jacob)

CHAPTER 12

VOCABULARY

CONDITIONAL WORDS

لَوْ	إِذَا	إِنْ
had...	when...	if...

WHERE ARE WE AT?
OF OCCURRENCES: ~1,100
% COVERED: 70%

ACTIONS

يَرْزُقُ	رَزَقَ	يُضِلُّ[15]	أَضَلَّ	يُحِبُّ[14]	أَحَبَّ
provides	provided	misguides	misguided	loves	loved

يَتْلُو[16]	تَلَا	يَصْبِرُ	صَبَرَ	يَنْصُرُ	نَصَرَ
recites	recited	is patient	was patient	helps	helped

يُخْرِجُ	أَخْرَجَ	يَخْرُجُ	خَرَجَ	يَقْضِي[17]	قَضَى
expels/ brings forth	expelled/ brought forth	leaves	left	judges/ decides	judged/ decided

WHERE ARE WE AT?
OF OCCURRENCES: ~580
% COVERED: 70%

SET PHRASES

بَيْنَ يَدَي/أَيْدِي
before/ahead of
(lit. between the hands)

CHAPTER 13-15
VOCABULARY

NOUNS

مُبِيْن	clear
رَحِيْم	merciful
حَكِيْم	wise
عَزِيْز	authoritative
ذُوْ – أُولُوْ*/أَصْحَاب	person of…
نَهَار	day
لَيْل	night
صَلَاة	prayer
نَبِيّ – أَنْبِيَاء/نَبِيُّوْن	prophet
زَوْج – أَزْوَاج	spouse/pair
وَلِيّ – أَوْلِيَاء	ally
فَضْل	favor

*note that أولوا can turn into أولي when it is a receiver or if it comes after a TLD word.

WHERE ARE WE AT?
OF OCCURRENCES: ~1,100
% COVERED: 71%

EXPRESSIONS OF CALLING

These phrases are used to grab the addressee's attention. They are most commonly followed by commanding actions, forbidding actions, or questions.

يَأَيُّهَا النَّاسُ	O, people!
يَأَيُّهَا الَّذِيْنَ ءَامَنُوْا	O you who believe!
رَبِّ/رَبَّنَا	My lord/Our lord!
يا قَوْمِ	My people!
اللَّهُمَّ	O God…
يا/يَأَيُّهَا	O…

WHERE ARE WE AT?
OF OCCURRENCES: ~420
% COVERED: 71.5%

CHAPTER 16
VOCABULARY

SEMI-EXPOSING WORDS

حَتَّى	لِكَيْ	لَنْ	أَنْ*
until...	in order to/so that...	will not...	to/that...

*note that when أَنْ is followed by a لا, the two words merge creating the word أَلَّا.

WHERE ARE WE AT?
OF OCCURRENCES: ~1,020
% COVERED: 73%

ACTIONS

يَتُوْبُ[20]	تَابَ	يُقِيْمُ[19]	أَقَامَ	يُرِيْدُ[18]	أَرَادَ
repents	repented	establishes	established	wants/intends	wanted/intended

يَدْعُوْ[21]	دَعَا	يَبْعَثُ	بَعَثَ	يَتُوْبُ (عَلَى)[20]	تَابَ (عَلَى)
calls	called	sends/resurrects	sent/resurrected	forgives	forgave

WHERE ARE WE AT?
OF OCCURRENCES: ~480
% COVERED: 73%

SET PHRASES

صِرَاط مُسْتَقِيْم
straight path

CHAPTER 17-19
VOCABULARY

ACTIONS

يَتَوَلَّى²⁴	تَوَلَّى		يَأْتِي²³	أَتَى		يَرَى²²	رَأَى
turns away	turned away		comes	came		sees	saw

يُلْقِي²⁷	أَلْقَى		يُوحِي²⁶	أَوْحَى		يَجْزِي²⁵	جَزَى
casts	cast		reveals	revealed		compensates	compensated

يُنَادِي³⁰	نَادَى		يُصِيبُ²⁹	أَصَابَ		يُطِيعُ²⁸	أَطَاعَ
calls out	called out		befalls	befell		obeys	obeyed

WHERE ARE WE AT?
OF OCCURRENCES: ~1,010
% COVERED: 74%

NOUNS

أَحَد/وَاحِد	عَالَمِيْن	إِنْسَان	وَجْه - وُجُوْه
one	creation	humans	face

مَاء	أَب - ءَابَاء	يَوْمَئِذٍ	يَوْم القِيَامَة
water	parent/forefathers	on that day	the day of standing

WHERE ARE WE AT?
OF OCCURRENCES: ~615
% COVERED: 75%

CH. 19 TEMPLATES

مَا كَانَ (X) لِ(Y)	مَا كَانَ لِ(X) أَنْ (Y)	كَفَى بِ(X) (Y)ًا	إِنْ...إِلَّا/ مَا...إِلَّا
X would not be one to Y	It would not be appropriate for X to Y	X suffices as Y	nothing but/only

WHERE ARE WE AT?
OF OCCURRENCES: ~415
% COVERED: 75.5%

CHAPTER 20

VOCABULARY

ACTIONS

يُدْخِلُ	أَدْخَلَ
admits	admitted

يُنْذِرُ	أَنْذَرَ
warns	warned

يُهْلِكُ	أَهْلَكَ
destroys	destroyed

يَفْتَرِي	افْتَرَى
fabricates	fabricated

يُعَلِّمُ	عَلَّمَ
teaches	taught

يُحَرِّمُ	حَرَّمَ
forbids	forbade

يَتَذَكَّرُ	تَذَكَّرَ
ponders	pondered

يَتَوَكَّلُ	تَوَكَّلَ
relies	relied

يُحْيِي	أَحْيَا
gives life	gave life

يَسْتَغْفِرُ	اسْتَغْفَرَ
seeks forgiveness	sought forgiveness

يَسْتَكْبِرُ	اسْتَكْبَرَ
is arrogant	was arrogant

يَسْتَطِيعُ[31]	اسْتَطَاعَ
is able	was able

WHERE ARE WE AT?	
# OF OCCURRENCES:	~530
% COVERED:	76%

SET PHRASES

أَلَمْ تَرَ
have you not heard of…?
have you not seen…?

CHAPTER 21

VOCABULARY

NOUNS

بَشَر	human
عَاقِبَة	outcome
سِحْر	magic
مِثْل	like
صَالِح – صَالِحُوْنَ*	good
بَيِّنَة - بَيِّنَات	clear proof
جَمِيْع/أَجْمَعُوْنَ	all
أَوَّل	first/earliest
وَيْل	woe
صَدْر - صُدُوْر	chest
دَار - دِيَار	home
شَهِيْد - شُهَدَاء	witness

*when this word comes in the feminine plural (صَالِحَات), it will usually have the meaning of "good deeds"

WHERE ARE WE AT?
\# OF OCCURRENCES: ~740
% COVERED: 77%

SET PHRASES

أَهْل الكِتاب	the people of the book (Jews and Christians)

CHAPTER 22

VOCABULARY

ADJECTIVES AND NOUNS

Remember, if you can spot 3 common letters between a word you know and a comparative, you can translate it.

قَدِيْر	بَصِيْر	سَمِيْع	خَبِيْر
capable	seeing	hearing	informed

غَفُوْر	الرَّحْمَن	رَحْمَة	سَلَام
forgiving	The Most Merciful	mercy	peace

WHERE ARE WE AT?
OF OCCURRENCES: ~500
% COVERED: 77.5%

ACTIONS

Remember, if you can spot 3 common letters between a word you know and a comparative, you can translate it.

يَظُنُّ ³⁴	ظَنَّ	يَضِلُّ ³³	ضَلَّ	يَمَسُّ ³²	مَسَّ
thinks	thought	strays	strayed	touches	touched

يُنَجِّي/يُنْجِي ³⁷	نَجَّى/أَنْجَى	يَرُدُّ ³⁶	رَدَّ	يَصُدُّ ³⁵	صَدَّ
saves	saved	returns	returned	averts	averted

WHERE ARE WE AT?
OF OCCURRENCES: ~290
% COVERED: 78%

CHAPTER 23

VOCABULARY

IDEAS

Remember that ideas are derived from actions. If you can spot 3 common letters with a word you know, you can translate the idea.

تَقْوَى	سُلْطَان	إِذْن	حَمْد
God consciousness	authority	permission	praise

شَهَادَة	حِكْمَة	مُلْك	مِيثَاق/عَهْد
testimony	wisdom	ownership	covenant

سُبْحَانَ	فِتْنَة	سُوْء	ضَلَال
glory be to…	trial	evil	misguidance

WHERE ARE WE AT?
OF OCCURRENCES: ~475
% COVERED: 79%

SET PHRASE

الَّذِينَ آمَنُوا وَعَمِلُوا الصَّالِحَاتِ
those who believe and do good

CHAPTER 24
VOCABULARY

COMPLEX NOUN STARTERS

The following words make up the first part of a complex noun.

مَا	الَّتِيْ	الَّذِيْنَ	الَّذِيْ
what/whatever	the one who (f)	the ones who	the one who

مَنْ
one who/whoever

WHERE ARE WE AT?
OF OCCURRENCES: ~3,300
% COVERED: 83%

COMPOUND WORDS

When the word مَا is preceded by certain TLD words, the two words merge.

مِمَّا	فِيْمَا	عَمَّا	بِمَا
from what	with regards to what	about what	because of

إِنَّمَا	أَنَّمَا	كُلَّمَا	كَمَا
only	that	whenever	just as

إِمَّا	أَمَّا
either…or	as for

WHERE ARE WE AT?
OF OCCURRENCES: ~850
% COVERED: 84%

CHAPTER 25

VOCABULARY

NOUNS

اِبْن - أَبْنَاء/بَنُوْن	child
أَخْ - إِخْوَان	brother
امْرَأَة - نِسَاء	woman
رَجُل - رِجَال	man
قَمَر	moon
شَمْس	sun
حِسَاب	accounting
أُمَّة	nation

WHERE ARE WE AT?	
# OF OCCURRENCES:	~425
% COVERED:	85%

ACTIONS

Present	Past	English
يَشْكُرُ	شَكَرَ	is grateful / was grateful
يَزِيدُ [38]	زَادَ	increases / increased
يَعْقِلُ	عَقَلَ	reasons / reasoned
يَنْسَى [40]	نَسِيَ	forgets / forgot
يَمُوتُ [39]	مَاتَ	dies / died
يَكْتُبُ	كَتَبَ	decrees/writes / decreed/wrote

WHERE ARE WE AT?	
# OF OCCURRENCES:	~280
% COVERED:	85%

CHAPTER 26

VOCABULARY

NOUNS

غَيْب	وَلَد - أَوْلَاد	قَرْيَة	نَذِيْر/مُنْذِر
unseen	child	town	warner

جِبَال	بَحْر	ظُلُمَات	نُوْر
mountains	sea	darkness	light

WHERE ARE WE AT?	
# OF OCCURRENCES:	~350
% COVERED:	85.5%

ACTIONS

شَهِدَ	يَشْهَدُ	حَسِبَ	يَحْسَبُ	حَكَمَ	يَحْكُمُ
witnessed	witnesses	thought	thinks	judged	judges

سَبَّحَ	يُسَبِّحُ	عَذَّبَ	يُعَذِّبُ	نَبَّأَ	يُنَبِّئُ
declared perfect	declares perfect	punished	punishes	informed	informs

WHERE ARE WE AT?	
# OF OCCURRENCES:	~260
% COVERED:	86%

VOCABULARY DRILLS

1) قَالَ – TO SAY

PAST

هُنَّ قُلْنَ	أَنْتَ قُلْتَ	أَنْتُمْ قُلْتُمْ	أَنْتِ قُلْتِ	أَنْتُنَّ قُلْتُنَّ
أَنْتُمَا قُلْتُمَا	أَنَا قُلْتُ	نَحْنُ قُلْنَا		

PRESENT BALD

هُوَ يَقُلْ	هِيَ/أَنْتَ تَقُلْ	أَنَا أَقُلْ	نَحْنُ نَقُلْ

COMMAND

أَنْتَ قُلْ	أَنْتُمْ قُولُوا	أَنْتِ قُولِي	أَنْتُنَّ قُلْنَ	أَنْتُمَا قُولَا

PAST PASSIVE   قِيْلَ

2) جَاءَ – TO COME

PAST

هُنَّ جِئْنَ	أَنْتَ جِئْتَ	أَنْتُمْ جِئْتُمْ	أَنْتِ جِئْتِ	أَنْتُنَّ جِئْتُنَّ
أَنْتُمَا جِئْتُمَا	أَنَا جِئْتُ	نَحْنُ جِئْنَا		

PRESENT BALD

هُوَ يَجِئْ	هِيَ/أَنْتَ تَجِئْ	أَنَا أَجِئْ	نَحْنُ نَجِئْ

PAST PASSIVE   جِيْءَ

3) هَدَى – TO GUIDE

PAST

هِيَ هَدَتْ	هُمْ هَدُوا

PRESENT BALD

هُوَ يَهْدِ	هِيَ/أَنْتَ تَهْدِ	أَنَا أَهْدِ	نَحْنُ نَهْدِ

4) آتَى – TO GIVE

PAST

هُمْ ءَاتَوْا	هِيَ ءَاتَتْ

COMMAND

أَنْتُمْ ءَاتُوْا	أَنْتَ ءَاتِ

PRESENT BALD

نَحْنُ نُؤْتِ	أَنَا أُوْتِ	هِيَ/أَنْتَ تُؤْتِ	هُوَ يُؤْتِ

PAST PASSIVE

أُوْتِيَ

5) أَخَذَ – TO TAKE

COMMAND

أَنْتُمْ خُذُوْا	أَنْتَ خُذْ

6) كَانَ – WAS

PAST

أَنْتُنَّ كُنْتُنَّ	أَنْتِ كُنْتِ	أَنْتُمْ كُنْتُمْ	أَنْتَ كُنْتَ	هُنَّ كُنَّ
		نَحْنُ كُنَّا	أَنَا كُنْتُ	أَنْتُمَا كُنْتُمَا

PRESENT BALD

نَحْنُ نَكُنْ	أَنَا أَكُنْ	هِيَ/أَنْتَ تَكُنْ	هُوَ يَكُنْ

COMMAND

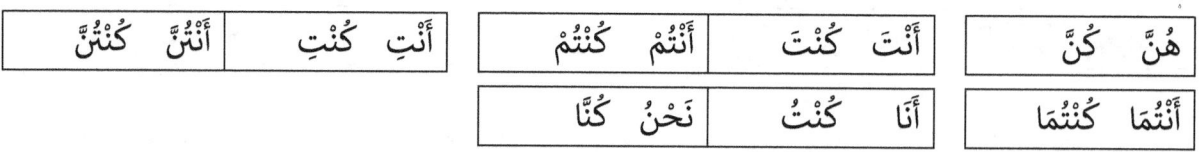

أَنْتُمَا كُوْنَا	أَنْتُنَّ كُنَّ	أَنْتِ كُوْنِيْ	أَنْتُمْ كُوْنُوْا	أَنْتَ كُنْ

7) كَادَ - ALMOST

PAST

هُنَّ كِدْنَ	أَنْتَ كِدْتَ	أَنْتُمْ كِدْتُمْ	أَنْتِ كِدْتِ	أَنْتُنَّ كِدْتُنَّ
أَنْتُمَا كِدْتُمَا	أَنَا كِدْتُ	نَحْنُ كِدْنَا		

PRESENT BALD

هُوَ يَكَدْ	هِيَ/أَنْتَ تَكَدْ	أَنَا أَكَدْ	نَحْنُ نَكَدْ

8) اِهْتَدَى – TO BE COMMITTED TO GUIDANCE

PRESENT BALD

هُوَ يَهْتَدِ	هِيَ/أَنْتَ تَهْتَدِ	أَنَا أَهْتَدِ	نَحْنُ نَهْتَدِ

9) رَضِيَ – TO BE PLEASED/TO PLEASE

PAST | هُمْ رَضُوا |

PRESENT BALD

هُوَ يَرْضَ	هِيَ/أَنْتَ تَرْضَ	أَنَا أَرْضَ	نَحْنُ نَرْضَ

10) أَكَلَ – TO EAT

COMMAND

أَنْتَ كُلْ	أَنْتُمْ كُلُوا	أَنْتِ كُلِي	أَنْتُمَا كُلَا

11) خَافَ – TO FEAR

PAST

هُنَّ خِفْنَ	أَنْتَ خِفْتَ	أَنْتُمْ خِفْتُمْ	أَنْتِ خِفْتِ	أَنْتُنَّ خِفْتُنَّ
أَنْتُمَا خِفْتُمَا	أَنَا خِفْتُ	نَحْنُ خِفْنَا		

PRESENT BALD

| نَحْنُ نَخَفْ | أَنَا أَخَفْ | هِيَ/أَنْتَ تَخَفْ | هُوَ يَخَفْ |

COMMAND | أَنْتُمْ خَافُوا |

12) شَاءَ – TO WILL, DESIRE

PAST

| أَنْتُنَّ شِئْتُنَّ | أَنْتِ شِئْتِ | أَنْتُمْ شِئْتُمْ | أَنْتَ شِئْتَ | هُنَّ شِئْنَ |
| | | نَحْنُ شِئْنَا | أَنَا شِئْتُ | أَنْتُمَا شِئْتُمَا |

PRESENT BALD

| نَحْنُ نَشَأْ | أَنَا أَشَأْ | هِيَ/أَنْتَ تَشَأْ | هُوَ يَشَأْ |

13) اِتَّقَى – TO BE CONSCIOUS OF

PAST

PRESENT BALD

| نَحْنُ نَتَّقِ | أَنَا أَتَّقِ | هِيَ/أَنْتَ تَتَّقِ | هُوَ يَتَّقِ |

COMMAND

| أَنْتُنَّ اِتَّقِينَ | أَنْتُمْ اِتَّقُوا | أَنْتَ اِتَّقِ |

14) أَحَبَّ – TO LOVE

PAST

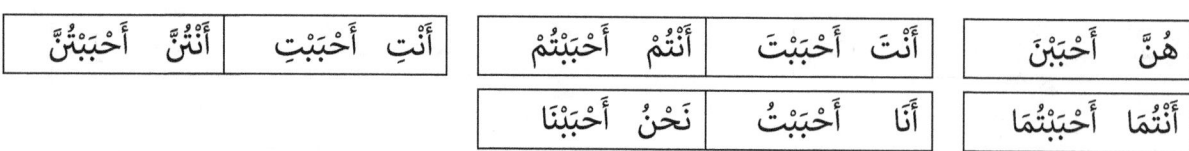

PRESENT BALD

| هُوَ يُحِبْ | هِيَ/أَنْتَ تُحِبْ | أَنَا أُحِبْ | نَحْنُ نُحِبْ |

15) أَضَلَّ – TO MISGUIDE

PAST

| هُنَّ أَضْلَلْنَ | أَنْتَ أَضْلَلْتَ | أَنْتُمْ أَضْلَلْتُمْ | أَنْتِ أَضْلَلْتِ | أَنْتُنَّ أَضْلَلْتُنَّ |
| أَنْتُمَا أَضْلَلْتُمَا | أَنَا أَضْلَلْتُ | نَحْنُ أَضْلَلْنَا | | |

PRESENT BALD

| هُوَ يُضْلِلْ | هِيَ/أَنْتَ تُضْلِلْ | أَنَا أُضْلِلْ | نَحْنُ نُضْلِلْ |

16) تَلَا – TO RECITE

PAST

| هُنَّ تَلَوْنَ | أَنْتَ تَلَوْتَ | أَنْتُمْ تَلَوْتُمْ | أَنْتِ تَلَوْتِ | أَنْتُنَّ تَلَوْتُنَّ |
| أَنْتُمَا تَلَوْتُمَا | أَنَا تَلَوْتُ | نَحْنُ تَلَوْنَا | | |

PRESENT BALD

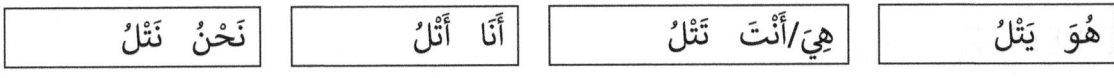

COMMAND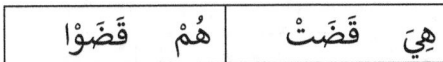

17) قَضَى – TO JUDGE/TO DECREE

PAST

| هِيَ قَضَتْ | هُمْ قَضَوْا |

PRESENT BALD

18) أَرَادَ – TO WANT/TO INTEND

PAST

أَنْتُنَّ أَرَدْتُنَّ	أَنْتِ أَرَدْتِ	أَنْتُمْ أَرَدْتُمْ	أَنْتَ أَرَدْتَ	هُنَّ أَرَدْنَ

نَحْنُ أَرَدْنَا	أَنَا أَرَدْتُ	أَنْتُمَا أَرَدْتُمَا

PRESENT BALD

نَحْنُ نُرِدْ	أَنَا أُرِدْ	هِيَ/أَنْتَ تُرِدْ	هُوَ يُرِدْ

19) أَقَامَ – TO ESTABLISH

PAST

أَنْتُنَّ أَقَمْتُنَّ	أَنْتِ أَقَمْتِ	أَنْتُمْ أَقَمْتُمْ	أَنْتَ أَقَمْتَ	هُنَّ أَقَمْنَ

نَحْنُ أَقَمْنَا	أَنَا أَقَمْتُ	أَنْتُمَا أَقَمْتُمَا

COMMAND

أَنْتُمْ أَقِيمُوا	أَنْتَ أَقِمْ

20) تَابَ – TO REPENT

PAST

أَنْتُنَّ تُبْتُنَّ	أَنْتِ تُبْتِ	أَنْتُمْ تُبْتُمْ	أَنْتَ تُبْتَ	هُنَّ تُبْنَ

نَحْنُ تُبْنَا	أَنَا تُبْتُ	أَنْتُمَا تُبْتُمَا

PRESENT BALD

نَحْنُ نَتُبْ	أَنَا أَتُبْ	هِيَ/أَنْتَ تَتُبْ	هُوَ يَتُبْ

COMMAND

أَنْتُمْ تُوبُوا	أَنْتَ تُبْ

21) دَعَا – TO CALL

PAST

هُنَّ دَعَوْنَ	أَنْتَ دَعَوْتَ	أَنْتُمْ دَعَوْتُمْ	أَنْتِ دَعَوْتِ	أَنْتُنَّ دَعَوْتُنَّ
أَنْتُمَا دَعَوْتُمَا	أَنَا دَعَوْتُ	نَحْنُ دَعَوْنَا		

PRESENT BALD

هُوَ يَدْعُ	هِيَ/أَنْتَ تَدْعُ	أَنَا أَدْعُ	نَحْنُ نَدْعُ

22) رَأَى – TO SEE

PAST

هِيَ رَأَتْ	هُمْ رَأَوْا

PRESENT BALD

هُوَ يَرَ	هِيَ/أَنْتَ تَرَ	أَنَا أَرَ	نَحْنُ نَرَ

23) أَتَى – TO COME

PAST

هِيَ أَتَتْ	هُمْ أَتَوْا

PRESENT BALD

هُوَ يَأْتِ	هِيَ/أَنْتَ تَأْتِ	أَنَا ءَاتِ	نَحْنُ نَأْتِ

COMMAND

أَنْتَ اِئْتِ	أَنْتُمْ اِئْتُوا

24) تَوَلَّى – TO TURN AWAY

PAST

| هِيَ تَوَلَّتْ | هُمْ تَوَلَّوْا |

PRESENT BALD

| هُوَ يَتَوَلَّ | هِيَ/أَنْتَ تَتَوَلَّ | أَنَا أَتَوَلَّ | نَحْنُ نَتَوَلَّ |

COMMAND | أَنْتَ تَوَلَّ |

25) جَزَى – TO COMPENSATE

PRESENT BALD

| هُوَ يَجْزِ | هِيَ/أَنْتَ تَجْزِ | أَنَا أَجْزِ | نَحْنُ نَجْزِ |

26) أَوْحَى – TO REVEAL

PRESENT PASSIVE BALD | هُوَ لَمْ يُوحَ |

27) أَلْقَى – TO CAST

PAST

| هِيَ أَلْقَتْ | هُمْ أَلْقَوْا |

COMMAND

| أَنْتَ أَلْقِ | أَنْتُمْ أَلْقُوا |

28) أَطَاعَ – TO OBEY

PAST

| هُنَّ أَطَعْنَ | أَنْتَ أَطَعْتَ | أَنْتُمْ أَطَعْتُمْ | أَنْتِ أَطَعْتِ | أَنْتُنَّ أَطَعْتُنَّ |
| أَنْتُمَا أَطَعْتُمَا | أَنَا أَطَعْتُ | نَحْنُ أَطَعْنَا |

PRESENT BALD

| هُوَ يُطِعْ | هِيَ/أَنْتَ تُطِعْ | أَنَا أُطِعْ | نَحْنُ نُطِعْ |

COMMAND   أَنْتُمْ أَطِيعُوا

29) أَصَابَ – TO STRIKE

PAST

| هُنَّ أَصَبْنَ | أَنْتَ أَصَبْتَ | أَنْتُمْ أَصَبْتُمْ | أَنْتِ أَصَبْتِ | أَنْتُنَّ أَصَبْتُنَّ |
| أَنْتُمَا أَصَبْتُمَا | أَنَا أَصَبْتُ | نَحْنُ أَصَبْنَا |

PAST PASSIVE   أُصِيبَ

30) نَادَى – TO CALL

PAST

| هِيَ نَادَتْ | هُمْ نَادَوْا |

PAST PASSIVE | هُوَ نُودِيَ | هُمْ نُودُوا |

31) اِسْتَطَاعَ – TO BE CAPABLE

PAST

| هُنَّ اِسْتَطَعْنَ | أَنْتَ اِسْتَطَعْتَ | أَنْتُمْ اِسْتَطَعْتُمْ | أَنْتِ اِسْتَطَعْتِ | أَنْتُنَّ اِسْتَطَعْتُنَّ |
| أَنْتُمَا اِسْتَطَعْتُمَا | أَنَا اِسْتَطَعْتُ | نَحْنُ اِسْتَطَعْنَا |

PRESENT BALD

| هُوَ يَسْتَطِعْ | هِيَ/أَنْتَ تَسْتَطِعْ/تَسْطِعْ | أَنَا أَسْتَطِعْ | نَحْنُ نَسْتَطِعْ |

32) مَسَّ – TO TOUCH

PRESENT BALD

_____   _____   _____   _____

PAGE | 9

| هُوَ يَمْسَسْ | هِيَ/أَنْتَ تَمْسَسْ | أَنَا أَمْسَسْ | نَحْنُ نَمْسَسْ |

33) ضَلَّ – TO BE MISGUIDED

PAST

هُنَّ ضَلَلْنَ	أَنْتَ ضَلَلْتَ	أَنْتِ ضَلَلْتِ
أَنْتُمَا ضَلَلْتُمَا	أَنَا ضَلَلْتُ	أَنْتُنَّ ضَلَلْتُنَّ
	أَنْتُمْ ضَلَلْتُمْ	
	نَحْنُ ضَلَلْنَا	

34) ظَنَّ – TO THINK

PAST

هُنَّ ظَنَنَّ	أَنْتَ ظَنَنْتَ	أَنْتِ ظَنَنْتِ
أَنْتُمَا ظَنَنْتُمَا	أَنَا ظَنَنْتُ	أَنْتُنَّ ظَنَنْتُنَّ
	أَنْتُمْ ظَنَنْتُمْ	
	نَحْنُ ظَنَنَّا	

35) صَدَّ – TO DIVERT

PAST

هُنَّ صَدَدْنَ	أَنْتَ صَدَدْتَ	أَنْتِ صَدَدْتِ
أَنْتُمَا صَدَدْتُمَا	أَنَا صَدَدْتُ	أَنْتُنَّ صَدَدْتُنَّ
	أَنْتُمْ صَدَدْتُمْ	
	نَحْنُ صَدَدْنَا	

PAST PASSIVE   هُمْ صُدُّوا

36) رَدَّ – TO RETURN

PAST

هُنَّ رَدَدْنَ	أَنْتَ رَدَدْتَ	أَنْتِ رَدَدْتِ
أَنْتُمَا رَدَدْتُمَا	أَنَا رَدَدْتُ	أَنْتُنَّ رَدَدْتُنَّ
	أَنْتُمْ رَدَدْتُمْ	
	نَحْنُ رَدَدْنَا	

COMMAND   أَنْتُمْ رُدُّوا

PAST PASSIVE   هُمْ رُدُّوا